BUNSOLOGY BODY

Sophia Perez King (SouLfia)

ISBN 978-1-63844-865-5 (paperback)
ISBN 978-1-63844-866-2 (digital)

Christian Faith Publishing
832 Park Avenue
Meadville, PA 16335
www.christianfaithpublishing.com

Printed in the United States of America

CONTENTS

INTRODUCTION

It all started in Fayetteville, North Carolina. Born into a blue-collar military family, father a Dominican soldier, and an amazing, beautiful, talented Indian and African American daughter of a music icon whose voice and body were larger than life. When I say larger than life, I literally mean five hundred pounds. So genetically, you already know the challenges I've had to endure with my health and weight. It was not until I realized that everything I felt my body was feeling, good and bad. You see, we are what we eat. Growing up in beauty pageants, the confidence was always there, and having all siblings be brothers and being an army brat, I've always been competitive, not knowing that I would one day deal with the insecurities of just simply being overweight or big-boned. However, what people perceive you to be is not what you and who you think you are.

Growing up as a child, I never realized that your health is your wealth until I graduated high school and moved to Los Angeles, California. The big city of dreams. I was granted a partial scholarship to AMDA (American Musical and Dramatic Academy) at the New York campus. Once I received my final acceptance letter, I called my grandfather and asked him for the balance of my tuition to attend AMDA. I later realized I wouldn't have any family there in New York, so I quickly called him back and said, "Hey, grandpa, I'll go there and help you move in, and I'll go to school in Calabasas. It's only a twenty-minute drive from Hollywood." He agreed; however, he didn't agree to pay the tuition to AMDA. He preferred for me to attend a state university to receive my bachelor's degree in communications and tour with him instead of going to school for music and acting. This was because he felt like that was a genetic gift that I would be able to develop as I toured the world with him. He always told me, "It's nothing like 'boots on the ground' training. Do you want to be in entertainment? Well, here you go!"

Within three months, I graduated high school. I was in Europe on tour on the road, singing, doing what I loved to do. Meanwhile, I was in college as well. It was a huge transition and a lot to handle. I was able to manage it all with the help of my family members, my tutor, and so much support from my mom and grandparents. My grandfather's tour manager Jane would always say, "Sophia, you're brilliant, you're beautiful, you can do all things you can do." Both of us were always on the go, out of the country for months at a time. I learned so much about health just simply being on the road with my grandfather. Imagine being five hundred pounds and having to travel every day to a new country or a new city, sometimes by airplane, sometimes tour buses, but always the best of everything that still didn't matter. I'm sure he was uncomfortable most of the time.

The moment I became his assistant, it completely changed my perception. And what I desired to do was to not only sing and heal and entertain the world but to be healthy myself and continue to help those in my family dealing with weight issues, insecurities, and low self-esteem. Although my grandfather had no issues with those, I knew he would have much rather been half his weight simply so he could drive, get up and go to the bathroom on his own, and do the simple things that we all do daily but take for granted. While helping my grandfather, I had an epiphany. I knew I wanted to help heal the world through health, fitness, and nutrition. You see, I traveled the world singing professional background with my grandfather and other famous singers such as Joss Stone, Aretha Franklin, Chaka Khan and toured with the pioneers of music. I was in a different country every day and never had energy. I realized that I had to do something about what I was putting into my body knowing that genetically I would struggle with weight challenges.

By the age of nineteen, I earned my first record deal. The first thing they said was, "We got to get her trainer. She's got to lose weight. She's got to come down. She's a bit too thick. She's a bit too heavy." I was always a little insecure about my weight. Even though I was a size 28, it still was too big for the career that I desired. It wasn't until I would push my grandfather around in a wheelchair going from country to country, performing on stages like the Glastonbury Festival, Bonnaroo, some of the biggest music festivals in the world, that I realized carrying all that weight is a job in itself. My grandfather registered for the Duke University weight loss program and lost twenty-two pounds. I learned so much through that process that it allowed me to understand the value in being healthy and feeling and looking your best.

Immediately following my college graduation in 2008, I signed a new record deal with Universal Republic/Brooklyn's Records. They said the same thing about my weight. I was never happy or content with my weight until about the age of twenty-two. I learned to accept my thick legs, booty, and curves. In the Summer of 2010, just before leaving Los Angles to head to Europe for three months, I met my husband. He was an NFL cornerback, and he was six-packed up, handsome, and everything I could possibly dream of. And his last name is King. Boy, was I happy to meet a king. My grandfather passed away, and we got closer and closer. We then got married, and I completely changed my eating habits. I changed everything from the portions to the kinds of meals we ate. Being on the road, you eat when you can and what you can. I've always been cautious about what I eat. I took it to the next level once I started seeing results in my body like a six-pack. You see, the great thing about transforming your body is actually physically seeing the change take place. You don't even desire or even have a taste for anything other than clean, healthy nutrients that energize your body and cleanse your mind and soul. Not only was I in love and wanted to help him transition from the NFL to real life, we completely fell in love with one another and began our life together.

I joined Herbalife, and it showed me that as long as you're feeding your cells and hydrating them with the proper nutrients, you can feel energized throughout the day and you can really do anything. Truly, nothing is impossible. I began my health journey when I was in high school, but it wasn't completely healthy. It was full of sugar and saturated fat, processed foods, and things that I would never eat today. I say all this to say it's never too late to transition into a new and healthier you.

Romans 12:1 says, "Therefore brothers and sisters I urge you in view of God's mercy to offer your bodies as a living sacrifice This is your true and proper worship." I didn't realize this until I became extremely ill. Doctors didn't know what was wrong. After being on tour with my grandfather for three months, I returned to Los Angeles, California, to find my face swollen on both sides and my jaws not producing enough saliva. Multiple doctors in the emergency room couldn't diagnose me. I remember one morning, I was sitting in solitude asking God to completely heal me and restore my beauty. I promised that I would live to please him and I would never take anything given for granted. You see, beauty is only skin deep. Our power is in our wisdom and our worship. Our freedom is in Jesus Christ.

> I will praise you for I am fearfully and won-
> derfully made, Miraculous are you works and
> that my soul know very well. (Psalm 134:14)

CHAPTER 1

Body: You Only Get One

Value your body; it's your temple. I always say be good to it because you only get one and you have to use it for the rest of your life.

I truly value God, myself, my family, and my health. Without health we have nothing. After one month of being ill, God finally healed me within days of that prayer. I'm guessing that was God showing me a miracle. I have to tell you that raw lemon freshly squeezed is the best healer. I gargled with raw lemon, and it opened my saliva glands in my cheeks. The swelling slowly disappeared. When they say natural remedies don't exist, don't believe them. Before antibiotics and all of these pills prescribed by doctors, all people had were fresh fruits, veggies, and raw honey. My lemon tree is my best friend. I never looked back. I also drink water all day, every day. I never drink alcohol, and I've never done drugs in my life after trying alcohol and marijuana at age thirteen with my big cousins. I never liked it. I didn't like the feeling of not being in control of how I felt. It didn't help that my dad was a military veteran and was a very heavy drinker.

We don't realize that up to 60 percent of the human adult body is water. According to H.H. Mitchell (Journal of Biological Chemistry 158), the brain and heart are composed of 73% water, and the lungs are about 83% water. The skin contains 64% water, muscles and kidneys are 79%, and even the bones are watery: 31%. So In general, you should try to drink between half an ounce and an ounce of water for each pound you weigh, every day." For example, if you weigh 150 pounds, that would be 75–150 ounces of water a day. Once I realized the power of water, I began to carry a gallon of water with me everywhere I went. Suddenly my energy levels changed. My body completely changed: my muscle and BMI increased, and I began to finally reach my goals. Fire and water are two very powerful things that God himself created. So remember, when you're not feeling well, sometimes it could simply be dehydration and/or lack of rest. Here are some basic ways to stay healthy without feeling overwhelmed with too many daily changes. Try to barely drink sugar calories like soda.

1. Eat nuts.
2. Avoid processed junk food (eat real food instead).
3. Don't fear coffee. Drink hot tea daily (green tea). When pregnant, drink milk thistle herbal tea.
4. Eat fatty fish.
5. Get enough sleep, at least eight hours.
6. Take care of your gut health with probiotics and fiber.
7. Drink plenty of water, especially before meals. I live by this motto. So moving forward, you know water heals, sugar kills, and salt fills you up.

Here is my list of twelve healthy daily habits that you can do every day to help create a healthier lifestyle:

1. Wake up early.
2. Drink water before anything else.
3. Make time for movement (exercise).
4. Spend time outside (vitamin D).

5.   Eat sitting down.
6.   Go for a walk.
7.   Take time to cook.
8.   Eat a vegetable daily.

While pregnant, always add these foods to your daily diet. Here are thirteen super nutritious foods to eat when you're pregnant to help make sure you're hitting those nutrient goals:

1.   Dairy products
2.   Legumes
3.   Sweet potatoes
4.   Salmon
5.   Eggs
6.   Broccoli and dark, leafy greens
7.   Lean meat and proteins
8.   Berries

I would never go more than an hour without drinking water while pregnant. Staying hydrated while pregnant is vital. I was never hungry for anything unhealthy because I stayed hydrated. I enjoy Green, veggies. Fruits and protein majority of the time. I realized that helped increase when I started nursing. The best foods to eat while nursing are calcium (milk, yogurt, cheese, leafy greens, legumes), iron (red meat, pork, poultry, seafood, beans, green vegetables, dried fruit), copper (shellfish, whole grains, nuts, beans, organ meats, potatoes), and zinc (oysters, red meat, poultry, beans, nuts, dairy). I would never go to sleep with a cold, chocolate Muscle Milk. Now I don't even drink it. My son weighed eight pounds and one ounce and was twenty-one and a half inches long.

Meanwhile, the worst foods to eat during pregnancy or nursing are

1. fish (high in mercury but a great source of docosahexaenoic acid (DHA) and eicosapentaenoic acid (EPA)—two types of omega-3 fatty acids that are important for brain development in infants yet can be hard to find in other foods);
2. some herbal supplements;
3. alcohol;
4. caffeine; and
5. highly processed foods.

I remember I used to love Special K cereal with a banana. Bananas are a high-calorie fruit that will help with hunger pangs while breastfeeding, and it helps to up your folic acid levels. What's more, potassium-packed bananas help nursing mums maintain their fluid and electrolyte levels, which can help maintain a good flow of breast milk. I had an overflow of milk for two years. My six-pack was ripped from nursing. I didn't use a waist trainer until my son was three months old. I was scared and wanted to allow my uterus to return to its normal size naturally. I knew I wanted another baby. Ladies, don't be so hard on yourself postpartum. Your body will thank you later. Allow your body to return to its natural state. Be easy on your uterus; it just held over 79 percent water in just its organs to help support your growing baby. It's so important to drink enough water while pregnant. Dehydration during pregnancy can lead to serious pregnancy complications including neural tube defects, low amniotic fluid, inadequate breast milk production, and even premature labor. These risks, in turn, can lead to birth defects due to a lack of water and nutritional support for your baby. I never experienced symptoms of gestational diabetes, but I have friends who have shared their experiences with me. If you have the symptoms below, please hydrate and get tested ASAP:

1. Increased thirst
2. Needing to pee more often than usual
3. A dry mouth
4. Tiredness

Remember, you must know your body and listen to your body. It will never lie to you. Whenever you ignore your body, it allows bacteria and bad viruses to easily form in our bodies. Regulating your immune system can influence our hormones and allow our bodies much more energy throughout the day. When you allow your body to heal naturally with simply changing your diet, hydration, and increasing your rest, it's proven that your lifespan will continue longer than the average sixty-eight years in the USA.

CHAPTER 2

What Should I Eat?

The deepest need of men is not food, clothes, or shelter, but what is as important is God. What a broad question "What should I eat?" People always ask this question. My answer is always, "Water, natural vitamins and nutrients from vegetables and fruits, and make sure you're getting enough protein." Veganism is an amazing way of life; however, your body must have at least three sources of protein. There are plenty meatless sources of protein as well. However, when I'm following this meal plan, I get extremely gassy. Remember, everybody's body is different. My favorite meatless sources of protein are nut butters, broccoli, seeds, beans, spinach, Greek yogurt, and oatmeal.

I enjoy fish; however, I do not eat beef or pork and never have since I was maybe in elementary school. It's been so long; I can't remember the last time I had something other than fish, ground turkey, or organic, boneless, skinless, white meat like chicken breast. However, most of the time, my protein comes from shakes and meatless sources. Once a day I'll do a green salad with a piece of grilled fish 99 percent of the time. When I have photo shoots or have to model or work on camera, I focus on hydrating with two protein shakes in one meal a day. This keeps me feeling light and lean. I do cardio five days a week and get in the steam room and sauna every day five days leading up to the shoot. This gives me that nice shred and gets off excess water retention. Throughout the COVID-19 pandemic, I was really sad I wasn't able to go to the steam room and sauna. The main reason I was able to lose lots of baby fat postpartum was because I worked out at home twice a week. The other three days I would go to the gym to do my abs in the steam room and sauna. It was also my time to meditate and pray. I enjoy going to the gym; it keeps me on a schedule and is the part of my day where I'm able to completely detox my mind as well as being nothing more than self-care. I feel like this is important for every woman every mother and everybody. Self-care is not selfish. I feel like everyone should have thirty to forty-five minutes a day when they just completely check no phone and simply meditate, pray, work out, and detox from the world.

My meal plan is as follows:
No carbs after 4:00 p.m.
2 bottles of water
1 lemon
1 cucumber
Fresh ginger
Fresh mint leaves
Visit Www.Bunsology.com

Meal Plan

Total calories: 1700 kcal
286 g carbs, 191 g protein, 70 g fat

1. Breakfast (Eat within 30 minutes of waking in addition to 1 cup of room-temperature water with freshly squeezed lemon.)
    a. 1 multivitamin *before* the meal with a large glass of water!
    b. *Large glass of water!*
    c. Oatmeal, boiled eggs or egg whites, or turkey bacon or sausage. If you take your shake for breakfast, there's no need to consume an actual meal listed above.
    d. You can also put in a spoonful of Greek yogurt, flax seeds, or a serving of no-sugar-added oatmeal to replace the almond butter or fruit.
2. Midmorning snack
    a. Eggs/egg whites with 1 cup of veggies and cayenne pepper and flax seeds with 1/4 cup oatmeal. Try to buy rolled oats—gluten free and higher in fiber and protein.
    b. Oatmeal with 1 tablespoon of cinnamon and 1 scoop of almond butter
    c. Almonds and an apple.
    d. Greek yogurt with almonds, cinnamon, etc.
3. Lunch (main meal)
    a. *Large glass of water!*
    b. 2 scoops of protein powder with 1/2 serving of fruit or 1 tablespoon of almond or peanut butter (raw and unsalted) and cinnamon. Mix with water or almond milk.
4. Midafternoon snack
    a. Greek yogurt with cucumber or celery.

    b.   1/2 sandwich on Ezekiel bread (low sodium) with turkey, tuna, chicken, and veggies. No dressings, but mustard is fine.

    c.   Lean meat with veggies and 1/3 sweet potato/yam or a brown rice cake.

    d.   Egg whites/lean meat with brown rice.

5. Midafternoon snack (Can be switched with any option from first midafternoon snack)

    a.   warm herbal/green tea

6. Dinner

    a.   *Large glass of water!*

    b.   Lean protein (chicken, fish, turkey, eggs) with veggies.

Berryfotogenicphotography.com

No carbs after 4:00 p.m. unless it's in the shakes!
Bunsology Body Guidelines

1. Drink at least one gallon of water per day.
2. No sugary drinks (sodas, juice, etc.)
    a. Vitaminwater Zero and sugar-free energy drinks are fine.
3. Do not add sugar or sweeteners to food.
    a. Agave, cane juice, etc. are *not* allowed
    b. Stevia, xylitol, and Splenda are fine (stevia and xylitol preferred, though.)
4. Food is not to be prepared with oil; a light amount of spray oil is fine.
5. No sauces or marinades that contain sugar and fat (lemon juice, lime juice, spices, nonfat chicken broth, etc. are fine).
6. *Avoid* cheat snacks (even tiny ones).
7. Meals should be eaten every three hours.
8. Take supplements that I've recommended only as directed (not more than suggested).
9. If you have a special event occasion wedding birthday, etc starting Monday morning get back to your regiment.
10. Be honest if you cheat on your diet. And drink lots of water to flush out the kidney.
11. Listen to your body. If you feel tired, overly hungry, etc., let me know so drink water with Lemon!
12. If ordering at a restaurant, make sure that they prepare your food with *olive oil* Spices, lemon juice, etc. are fine. The brand I use is from herbalife but feel free to find.
13. Food choice list is provided; you may substitute foods, but be sure to match up macronutrients accordingly if you do so.
14. Take your *cellulose* three times a day. Take your cell activator and your multivitamin three times daily with shakes and/or meals.

As of right now, what we're trying to do is boost your metabolism; therefore, we are going to have five meals a day with pretty balanced micronutrients.

Micronutrients are essential elements required by organisms in varying quantities throughout life to orchestrate a range of physiological functions to maintain health. You absolutely need them to be at your best health as a whole. Micronutrients are the elements required by us in small quantities. Iron, cobalt, chromium, iodine, copper, zinc, and molybdenum are some of the micronutrients. There are sixteen elements essential to the growth of crop plants:

1. Supplied by air and water: carbon, hydrogen, oxygen
2. Macronutrients: nitrogen, phosphorous, potassium
3. Secondary Nutrients: calcium, magnesium, sulfur
4. Micronutrients: boron (B), chlorine (Cl), copper (Cu), iron (Fe), manganese (Mn), molybdenum (Mo), and zinc (Zn)

But when you're pregnant or nursing your babies, the most important micronutrients for babies before birth are folic acid, vitamin A, iron, iodine, and omega-3 fatty acid docosahexaenoic acid (DHA). These vitamins are called micronutrients because your body needs only tiny amounts of them. Yet failing to get even those small quantities virtually guarantees disease. I say this because nutritionists like myself spend a lot of time discussing total digestible nutrients, minerals, crude protein, and even various fractions of protein. However, we often take for granted the most important nutrient, the one required in the greatest amount by any class of livestock: water. Water is the most healing source in the world. To make sure you're getting enough nutrients, make sure you try to eat a variety of foods to get different vitamins and minerals. Foods that naturally are nutrient-rich include fruits and vegetables. Lean meats, fish, whole grains, dairy, legumes, nuts, and seeds also are high in nutrients. Not only do we need micronutrients; we also need macronutrients. Micronutrients are the nutrients your body needs in smaller amounts, which are commonly referred to as vitamins and minerals.

We need macronutrients to help with energy, and we need micronutrients to help our body be healthy and digest those macronutrients. So both are extremely important. However, water is the most important because you must flush everything out through your kidneys with water.

CHAPTER 3

No Hood Like Motherhood

However, I braced becoming a mom. It was something I always desired. My husband of five years was so excited and couldn't wait. It is very true what they say: you are never prepared. All the books in the world can never prepare you for the most life-altering part of every woman's life: motherhood. Not only did my body change; my metabolism changed. The foods that I enjoyed changed, and everything I ate when I was pregnant, including ramen noodles and Thai food, I couldn't stand postpartum. But I do tell you, this being-pregnant food never tasted so good. In the last three months of pregnancy, you will gain the most weight, but remember, most of it is water retention. You will be visually shed once the baby is born. Like I said in previous chapters, I gained thirty-eight pounds and was able to lose it all by my fourth month and get back to my thick body. Eventually, by eight months, I had my six-pack back. One of the main factors to naturally losing weight faster postpartum is nursing. Breastfeeding burns up to five hundred calories a day. This means that even though you are probably eating more to sustain breastfeeding, you can still lose weight. On average, if you're taking in the recommended amount of calories each day and breastfeeding exclusively, you should lose about one pound every week or two. Beyond providing nourishment and helping to protect your baby from getting sick, breastfeeding can also help you lose weight gained during pregnancy. When you breastfeed your baby, you use fat cells stored in your body during pregnancy—along with calories from your diet—to fuel your milk production and feed your baby.

Nursing is one of the most rewarding parts of being a new mommy. You're able to transfer all-natural vitamins and minerals directly from your body straight to your baby. I nursed my son until he was nineteen months old. I tried to go two years, but he got too many teeth and was just so big. I was never able to go out or be away from him for more than two to three hours. He was my first baby, so I was extra attached to him. I would not advise anyone to do this. My son wouldn't take a bottle; he was always on my hip. Which equals a spoiled baby and a tired mommy. I realized that there are so many ways of being a healthy mom, and in return for being a healthy mom, your family will be healthy.

Remember, they eat what you cook and you're the leader in the kitchen. These are the foods to limit or avoid while breastfeeding:

1. Fish (high in mercury)
2. Some herbal supplements
3. Alcohol
4. Caffeine
5. Highly processed foods

I say this because everything you're eating is being digested and transferred to your baby, as well as spicy food. The Bible says your body is your temple and that you should treat as such. Nutrition is simply a lifestyle. No diet works unless we work and actually follow through with it each day.

> Her children rise up and Call her blessed and
> her husband many women have done excellently
> but you surpass them all. (Proverbs 31:28–31)

CHAPTER 4

Diets

I personally am not a complete vegan; however, for some people, their bodies need to follow the structured vegan diet to detox, cleanse, stay healthy, and lose weight as well as fight off disease. However, there are three forms of protein. Protein is the basic component of living cells and is made of carbon, hydrogen, oxygen, nitrogen, and one or more chains of amino acids. The three types of proteins are fibrous, globular, and membrane. Here are the seven forms of protein:

1. Whey protein (Whey protein comes from milk.)
2. Casein Protein (Like whey, casein is a protein found in milk.)
3. Egg protein
4. Pea protein
5. Hemp protein
6. Brown rice protein
7. Mixed plant proteins

But it's important to eat the right amount and the right kind of protein to get its health benefits. Here are different sources of protein:

1. Seafood. Seafood is an excellent source of protein because it's usually low in fat.
2. White meat (poultry). Stick to the white meat from poultry for excellent, lean protein.
3. Milk, cheese, and yogurt. I only eat Greek yogurt. I'm lactose intolerant, so I use almond milk. I feel like everybody has a different digestive system. Some people's bodies are fine with dairy; mine will completely blow up. So I'm a non-dairy, fish, turkey, and chicken breast lover. I also love egg whites.
4. Eggs. I never eat yolk. But when I was pregnant, they forced me to. Babies' brains need the whole egg. I don't believe in depriving your body of natural sources and forms of protein. A balanced diet is far more important than just staying vegan and eating a bunch of carbs or beans. Below is a complete vegan meal plan for the vegan mom postpartum. Water will be your best friend.

Dr. Mark Hymond
Healthy fats
Processed carbs
Carbs burn

Is there like kindling on a fire; they burn quickly and then go out dropping your blood sugar and creating severe cravings: the physical signal that your body needs more fuel. To keep your metabolism burning, you must constantly eat more, and then you crash. And then you eat more, and then you crash. See how carbs like bread, pasta, rice, and, yes, even whole-grain affects your blood sugar? Protein has a much lower response. It will raise blood sugar a small amount, like fat. Take a look at that. Almost no rise in blood sugar at all. When you eat fat, it's like putting logs in the fire. What you get is just a long, steady source of fuel, and that's one of the reasons that I like a low-carb diet so much. It's because they don't fire if you're home or going up to the sky every time that you eat and then crashing down and making you if that's not happening. It's much easier to not overeat. Feeling fuller with fewer carbs and a higher amount of fats and protein.

Fats, healthy fats, are great for your entire body.

Low-fat dieters need to remember the body requires some healthy fats to maintain the immune system, regulate vital organs, and keep good cholesterol levels up. They also help regulate insulin levels, which make you feel more satisfied after a meal than consuming protein and carbs alone," Eede says.

Rachel Minton once said that for every complex problem, there is a solution that is simple and clear. The biggest scam ever perpetrated among the American people is this whole notion of cholesterol. I watering the lucrative to keep this idea going that we need to lower cholesterol has definitely become the bogeyman of cardiology, and here's what's so interesting about cholesterol. We need it. Our bodies cannot exist without it, yet due to simplistic thinking, we try and lump cholesterol into either good cholesterol or bad cholesterol and want to lower the bad cholesterol (the LDL) while raising the good cholesterol. That is incredibly simplistic. It turns out that raising your LDL cholesterol through diet does not translate into heart attacks and death. It just doesn't. When you take cholesterol Advil, just see if people who are saturated actually have a higher chance of dying. Do they actually become more prone to heart disease? That's what we care about. Let's take that out of the equation and see what the result is, which is what we care about. And every time they do that between the amount of fat you eat in your diet and getting hard, we now know the chronic inflammation caused by a diet high in sugar, refined grains, and refined best lawyers is far more dangerous to our health.

Atherosclerosis is an inflammatory disease. It's not a buildup of fat in the artery; it's actually an inflammation. The clash of them will go to that damage to try to repair it, but it didn't cause the damage. The damage has to come first. That's like saying that firefighters caused the fire when they just turned up to put the fire out. They were there by association, but they were there to repair, not call home. Inflammation is probably the number one promoter of every disease. The number one inflammatory substance in American: sugar. That's it. I mean, you put those two things together: inflammation makes everything worse, and sugar is the number one inflammatory substance we consume.

Sugar is your worst enemy! Over time, this can lead to a greater accumulation of fat, which may turn into fatty liver disease, a contributor to diabetes, which in turn raises your risk for heart disease. Consuming too much added sugar can raise blood pressure and increase chronic inflammation, both of which are pathological pathways to heart disease. When you eat excess sugar, the extra insulin in your bloodstream can affect your arteries all over your body. It causes their walls to get inflamed, grow thicker than normal, and become more stiff. This stresses your heart and damages it over time. This can lead to heart diseases like heart failure, heart attacks, and strokes. I always have to drink plenty of water if I eat something with too much sugar. My mouth gets dry, and I feel tired. I know right away if I've had too much sugar. Now in my thirties, I wonder how I was able to digest the sugar I used to eat. Unbelievable how the nutrition industry made us think sugar was okay and fat was bad for you. Anything low in fat is processed and refined. As I became a Cerritos nutritionist, I realized that sugar was worse than fat. Don't be fooled by the box that says "low-fat." It's actually worse than the natural product. Low fat doesn't mean healthy. In college I used to love cheese. I always bought the reduced-fat cheese. Now I realize that the regular cheeses are actually healthier than those with reduced fat or those processed even more and with added sugar, which is worse than fat. Healthy fats are really great for you. Healthy fats are found in the following:

1. Avocados (The avocado is different from most other fruits.)
2. Cheese (Cheese is incredibly nutritious.)
3. Dark chocolate (Dark chocolate is one of those rare health foods that actually tastes incredible.)
4. Whole eggs
5. Fatty fish
6. Nuts
7. Chia seeds
8. Extra virgin olive oil

All these fats are natural and completely safe and healthy for your cells and body to digest. You can't outrun your fork. Basically, you can't work out and eat dirty. You must eat clean and lean. Fats are not the problem. Sugar is the issue. Remember, food at its most natural state is much better than overcooking anything. Play macronutrients and shoot for the ratio of carbohydrate, protein, and fat used. The important point is there are essential fats and essential proteins, but there are no essential carbohydrates. Essential means the nutrients are required to sustain human life. We must eat this to survive, but there is no physical or biological need for us to consume any carbohydrates at all. Keto is the best way for your body to be. Eating fats speeds up your metabolism; carbs slow down your metabolism.

Omega-3 fatty acids, protein, iron, zinc, iodine, calcium, and vitamin D are all nutrients that could be lacking in a vegan diet. Vegan food sources of these nutrients include the following:

1. Protein: nuts, seeds, beans, legumes, tofu, seitan, tempeh, quinoa, buckwheat, and amaranth
2. Omega-3 fatty acids: flax oil and ground flax seeds, walnuts, soy, algae, foods fortified with DHA
3. Iodine: iodized salt and sea vegetables such as nori
4. Iron: lentils, kidney beans, black beans, dark leafy greens, raisins, and fortified grains
5. Calcium: dark leafy greens, tofu, baked beans, almonds, sesame seeds, figs, fortified soy milk, and almond milk
6. Zinc: fortified grains, some veggie burgers, kidney beans, black-eyed peas, peanuts, tempeh, tofu, tahini
7. Vitamin D: sunlight and fortified dairy alternatives

Vegan diets do not provide sufficient vitamin B12; therefore, supplementation is usually recommended. Check with your healthcare professional.

When pregnant and breastfeeding, the need for certain nutrients increases to support your health and your baby's. If you are in either of these stages, here are other nutrients to be aware of in your diet:

1. Folate: lentils, pinto beans, asparagus, spinach, black beans, broccoli
2. Vitamin B6: sweet potato, white potato, sunflower seeds, spinach, banana
3. Choline: collard greens, brussels sprouts, broccoli, swiss chard, cauliflower, spinach
4. Vitamin A (extra is needed when breastfeeding): sweet potato, carrots, spinach, kale, mustard greens, turnip greens, swiss chard, winter squash

Selecting meals and snacks from the options listed below (all vegan!) will help you meet your intake of important nutrients.

Breakfast

1. Quinoa drizzled with coconut milk, topped with chopped almonds and berries
2. Rolled oats made with fortified soy or almond milk and mixed with walnuts and raisins
3. Smoothie made with fortified soy or almond milk, ground flax seeds, berries, spinach, nut butter, and brewer's yeast
4. Avocado toast on whole grain bread with veggies and spices, a piece of fruit, and a glass of plant-based milk
5. Amaranth topped with chia seeds and chopped figs

Lunch

1. Quinoa mixed with shredded nori, sesame seeds, and black beans.
2. Scrambled tofu with brewer's yeast, salsa (or other seasoning), and chopped kale and bell pepper. Serve over a bed of brown rice.
3. Pilaf with lentils and grain of choice (bulgur, quinoa, farro, etc.) with squash.
4. Baked falafel with roasted sweet potato wedges and a side salad.
5. Veggie burger on a whole grain bun and a baby kale salad with chopped figs.

Dinner

1. Quinoa or bean-based pasta, spaghetti sauce with chopped seitan, sautéed kale
2. Grilled tofu or tempeh with fresh veggies, Asian-style dressing, and brown rice
3. Spicy sautéed tofu and veggies over buckwheat noodles
4. Baked seasoned tofu, buckwheat, and roasted vegetables

5. Acorn squash stuffed and baked with black beans, quinoa, walnuts, chopped figs, and spinach

Snacks

1. Fruit smoothie made with almond milk and added ground flax seeds
2. Trail mix: raisins, figs, almonds, and walnuts
3. Carrots and hummus (made with tahini)
4. Corn and avocado salsa with kidney beans, and whole-grain tortilla chips on the side
5. Chia seed pudding: fortified almond milk, chia seeds, vanilla, and berries

The questions I get asked all the time are, "How did you get a six-pack?" "How do you maintain it?" and "How did you get it back naturally after giving birth to an eight-pound-one-ounce, twenty-one–and-a-half inch baby boy?" My answer is always the same: 99 percent nutrition. I have never been an alcohol drinker. I have never done drugs of any form. I tried marijuana at fourteen and didn't like the feeling to the munchies. I'm a control freak, and I love to be able to control how I feel at all times. Below are eight proven ways to lose belly fat and live a healthier lifestyle:

1. Try curbing carbs instead of fats.
2. Think about an eating plan, not a diet.
3. Keep moving.
4. Lift weights. Do not be afraid to lift. Having muscle equals more energy. You burn more calories the more muscle you have.
5. Become a label reader. It's so important to know what you're putting into your body. I never really get to keep up with my calorie intake, but I know if it's not lean and green, it's not clean.
6. Move away from processed foods. Nothing in the middle aisle of the grocery store. Everything on the perimeter has

green veggies and protein. If it's in a box, it's processed and packaged.

7. Focus on the way your clothes fit more than reading a scale. Muscle weighs more than fat. It's about how you feel, how lean you are, and how much muscle you gain.

8. Hang out with health-focused friends. I'm only around people who are my equal or better. If we can fill one another's cups, then I don't need it. You are who you associate yourself with.

I can't say this five-letter word more than enough: *water*. Water is the way. God created it. It's the only thing that can take out fire. Water is powerful and can heal everything and anything. Want to lose or gain weight? Water is always the answer. I also can promise you that you can lose belly fat if you follow these effective tips(backed by science):

1. Eat plenty of soluble fiber. Foods containing high levels of soluble fiber include dried beans, oats, oat bran, rice bran, barley, citrus fruits, apples, strawberries, peas, and sweet potatoes. Oats are high in soluble fiber, making oat cereals a better choice than bran for this particular dietary component. A bowl of oatmeal made from 3/4 cup of dry oats contains 3 grams of soluble fiber.
2. Avoid foods that contain trans fats. Some examples are chips, pretzels, and other processed snacks.
3. Don't drink too much alcohol.
4. Eat a high-protein diet.
5. Reduce your stress levels.
6. Don't eat a lot of sugary foods.
7. Do aerobic exercise (cardio).
8. Cut back on carbs, especially refined carbs. Bunsology guidelines state *no* carbs after 4:00 p.m., only greens.

Now that you are pregnant, here is the time to eat, rest, relax, and love yourself and your mate. If you're alone when pregnant, that's okay because we are actually never alone. God is always with us; he provides everything for us and loves and forgives us before we even fall. Find the time to spend with God during this time. Remember, forty weeks go by so fast and most women do not carry the entire 40 weeks. Here is a list of things not to do while pregnant:

1. Alcohol.
2. Caffeine.
3. Overheating.
4. Contact sports.
5. Fall.
6. Amusement parks.
7. Smoking.

8. Changing the litter box.
9. Heavy lifting.
10. Drugs.
11. And if you have not been working out really hard, don't start going crazy in the gym unless you were doing it prior to pregnancy.

The health and well-being of both the woman and the developing fetus are of primary concern during pregnancy, so it's best to avoid consuming certain foods and doing potentially risky activities. I'm actually not an alcohol drinker; however, I do like a glass of wine every now and then. I realize that relaxes me. Red wine also contains antioxidants that can boost the immune system, increase bone density, reduce the risk of stroke, reduce the risk of heart disease, can lower cholesterol, and reduce the risk of type 2 diabetes. People always ask me, "Can you drink red wine daily?" I say for most people, enjoying a glass or two of red wine each day can be a part of the helpful diet; however, I don't do it every day. Just once in a while. The key is moderation regardless of the possible health, and if it's drinking, excessive alcohol can do more harm than good.

People always ask how I got a six-pack and how I maintained it. They think my lifestyle must be really strict, but it actually really is. I am a plain eater, and my husband always says that I'm boring; everything is lean or green for me. However, I do have my favorite things to drink like chai tea latte, which is loaded with sugar. And I love hot tea. I'm a singer, so I can drink a cup of hot tea instead of eating at any moment. This is why intermediate fasting is a way of life for me. It works for me, and I advise it to many women trying to change their lifestyle instead of dieting. I don't believe in diets. When I was in college, one of my friends told me my diet was "die time" because it was like I was starving myself and killing myself internally, which, when I look back now, I realize I really was. I get this question all the time: "Why do I gain weight in my stomach only?" A lot of women don't understand gaining weight solely in the stomach may be the result of specific lifestyle choices. The cause is stress, and sugar plays a significant role in the size of your midsection. Certain medical conditions and hormonal changes can contribute to abnormal weight gain as well. A college friend of mine would always say, "Why does my stomach look pregnant?" So when you have a six-pack but you don't eat, explain to her Indo belly can cause discomfort, pain, and pressure in your and your back. The lower abdomen can swell for days, weeks, or just a few hours. Many women who experience Indo belly say that they look pregnant even though they're not. This is just a synonym for enormous, excessive belly fat. This excess is extremely unhealthy; it is a risk factor of diseases like metabolic syndrome, type 2 diabetes, heart disease, and cancer. The medical term for unhealthy fat in the belly is *visceral fat*, which refers to fats around the liver and other organs in your abdomen. To get rid of your stomach, it is important to eat plenty of soluble fiber and avoid foods that contain trans fat. Don't drink too much alcohol, eat a high-protein diet, reduce your stress levels, don't eat a lot of sugary foods, do aerobic exercise, which is cardio, and cut back on carbs, especially refined carbs. There are short-term ways to reduce belly fat. For instance, for seven days, you can include cardio to your daily exercise routine, reduce refined carbs, add fatty fish to your diet, start the day with a high-protein breakfast, drink a lot of water, reduce your salt intake, and consume soluble fiber.

If your stomach is big and you're not pregnant, your stomach may swell up and feel hard. The explanation is as simple as overeating or drinking carbonated drinks. Remember, other cases may be more serious such as inflammatory bowel disease. Sometimes accumulated gas from drinking a soda too quickly can result in a hard stomach. There are many reasons why people gain belly fat, including a poor diet, lack of exercise, and stress. Improving nutrition, increasing activity, reducing stress, and making other lifestyle changes can all help people lose unwanted belly fat.

Belly fat refers to fat around the abdominal area. It's important to check your stomach for pregnancy, especially when you're trying to conceive. Walk your fingers up the side of your abdomen until you feel the top of your abdomen under the skin. It will feel like a hard ball. If you can feel the top of you're the top by curving your fingers gently in the diamond with the woman lying on her back being by finding the top of the uterus with your fingers. Or simply take a pregnancy test and find out for certain. The worst thing to do is to not know and not take your vitamins and eat properly. Many women also notice an increase in belly fat as they get older even if they aren't gaining weight. This is likely due to decreasing levels of estrogen, which appears to influence where fat is distributed in the body. Running or walking as your exercise burns calories, and your body's fat percentage decreases. So exercising not only helps you reduce belly fat, it also sheds fat from other areas. Running and walking are two of the best fat-burning exercises that can flatten your stomach naturally. Cut calories but not too much. Eat more fiber especially psyllium fiber. Take probiotics. Do some cardio. Drink protein shakes. Eat foods with monounsaturated fatty acids, then monitor your intake of carbs, especially refined carbs. Do resistance training. If you don't have time to do resistance training, there are ways to reduce your tummy without exercise. Drinking coffee equals weight loss. Or herbal tea. Since I'm not a coffee drinker, herbal tea works perfectly for me. Having herbal tea with no sugar, you get enough shut-eye. It's true, lack of sleep does contribute to weight gain, so make sure you get eight hours at night. To hit maximum chill, first things first: chill out and relax. Take a bath, dine on dark chocolate, work on your posture, drink some lemon water, do not chew gum. Make sure you're getting plenty of water. Green tea is great. Black tea and green tea help stimulate weight loss. Drink lots of water (I can't stress this enough). Consume apple cider vinegar drinks, high-protein drinks, and vegetable juice.

There are also many ways to help get rid of a bloated belly quickly. Go for a walk, try yoga poses, use peppermint capsules. I try gas-relief capsules such as Thermo-bond from Herbalife. You can also try abdominal massages using essential oils and take a warm bath, soaking and relaxing.

Bloating is when your belly feels swollen after eating. It is usually caused by excessive gas production or a disturbance in the movement of the muscles of the digestive system. Bloating can cause pain, discomfort, and a stuffed feeling. It can also make your stomach look bigger. Bloating occurs in the abdominal area. It happens when amounts of air or gas build up in the gastrointestinal track. Eating is a common cause of bloating because when the body digests food, it produces gas. I'm a firm believer in drinking plenty of water and tea. While I was pregnant and even while nursing, I realized that at night, if I get hungry, Muscle Milk or a small protein shake would suppress my appetite, help me lose weight, and help me feel full at the same time. And I still get in the protein and micronutrients my body needed to stay healthy. But when I was in college and knew nothing about nutrition, I ate Cheez-It Crackers and dry cereal. I stayed gassy and bloated all the time. I was always hungry and never gave my body the proper nutrients it needed. It wasn't until I turned twenty-two when I realized my body was my temple and that I had to be very careful what I fed it. I instantly saw a change in my body. I joined the group workouts, and by the time I turned twenty-four, I joined Herbalife, which completely changed my life and my perception of food, micronutrients, and the body in general. I took supplementation, natural supplements of cellulose and amino acids, and I've never taken any form of diet pills because I'm too scared. You

can't even get me to take a Tylenol or any over-the-counter medications. I don't like feeling like I can't control my body. I'm also afraid to get addicted because I do have an addictive personality, so I'm careful what I feed my body. It's crazy because when I look back to when I was younger, I wish I knew then what I know now. I'd probably live to be a hundred years plus, but my health journey begin in my mid-twenties. It's not that bad; some people wait until their thirties or forties or maybe fifties to even start to eat right. I've been eating right for more than a decade, so it's not so bad. I learned that one of the healthiest foods in the world is so cheap. It's spinach. *Spinach.* This nutrient-dense green superfood is readily available—fresh, frozen, or even canned. Being one of the healthiest foods on the planet, spinach is packed with energy while being low in calories, and it provides vitamin A, vitamin K, and essential folate. Meanwhile, some of the healthiest foods are my favorites and are ones I eat daily. I would advise every woman trying to conceive or simply just trying to stay healthy and fit to include at least three of these in their daily meal:

1. Fruits, vegetables, and berries.
2. Broccoli. Broccoli provides good amounts of fiber, calcium, potassium, folate, and phytonutrients.
3. Apples. Apples are an excellent source of antioxidants, which combat free radicals.
4. Kale.
5. Blueberries.
6. Avocados.
7. Leafy green vegetables.
8. Sweet potatoes.

Although sweet potatoes are my favorite, you will never catch me eating potato chips. french fries, or any form of potato. I really don't like potatoes; however, I enjoy sweet potatoes alongside a great piece of fish and veggies. But regular potatoes, french fries, or potato chips, I've never been a fan of. Another cool fact about me is that I don't eat fried foods. Because fried foods are high in fat, calories, and often salt. A few studies, including one published in 2014, have linked fried foods to serious health problems like type 2 diabetes and heart disease. Meanwhile, the worst foods you can consume are sugary drinks, most pizzas, white bread, most fruit juices, sweetened breakfast cereals, fried/grilled/broiled food, pastries, cookies, and cakes.

And I would never advise anyone to eat any of these foods. Actually, in college I had to do a project on hotdogs. Once I realized hotdogs were made out of a left over scraps, I couldn't understand how people can actually eat the scraps of anything. This is why I've never been a fan of pork.

1. H ot dogs. Processed meats in general are just one of the worst things you can put into your body.
2. Pretzels. Pretzels are the ultimate "wolf in sheep's clothing" type of food.
3. Diet soda. Just because something is calorie-free doesn't mean it's chemical-free.
4. Processed pastries.
5. Fluorescent orange snacks.

Most people think that they are healthy if they are vegan. That is not always true. Most vegan foods and products also include things like dipotassium phosphate, potassium chloride, titanium dioxide, and maltodextrin. Are the chemicals in fake meat harmful? Probably not. But many people want to avoid them anyway.

I do my best to avoid anything processed. I do love miso soup, and it has tofu in there and seaweed. I enjoy a cup of miso soup probably every week, which I probably should limit because of the sodium intake. But you learn your body is in order at 34 hours. I realize that I can always learn more about my body, but my body changes every single day. The only thing constant in the world is change. After all, God created each of us perfectly, and we are wonderfully made in his own image. So we are perfect to God. Things biblically I realize that there is a reason for every season and everything the most humbling time of my life as when I was pregnant. I realize that women literally have superpowers and are superhuman; we can create life.

CHAPTER 5

Different Types of Diets

So here we are. I remember my very first diet. I was in high school. I was competing in the state pageant for the state of North Carolina, not realizing that I'm a kid and have baby fat and that it would eventually go away the more active I became. Throughout my high school years, the more defined and lean my body became. The younger we are the faster we can gain muscle, and we burn fat much more swiftly because of our age. Around thirteen, my health became more important to me. I was more in tune about what I was eating, and then I realized your health is your wealth. Fourteen years later, I met my husband, a retired NFL player whose body was completely ripped. He had a six-pack. Actually, a twelve-pack! I mean, he was everything that I dreamed of in a man and more; however, his diet wasn't the best. He worked out eight hours a day and practiced six days a week, but he ate what he wanted. And his body was still completely shredded. I didn't understand how or why that could be, but little do we all know, everyone's body is different. The older we get the less calories we burn naturally. I learned that diets can be "die time." I say this because a lot of people think that starving themselves and consuming less calories leads to losing weight and being healthy. Not true. There are so many diets; the list can go on and on. Below I have listed a few that I know have helped me and numerous clients of mine as well as professional athletes.

Here are some of the recommendations according to the "Eat Right for Your Type" diet:

1. Those with type O blood should choose high-protein foods and eat lots of meat, vegetables, fish, and fruit but limit grains, beans, and legumes. To lose weight, seafood, kelp, red meat, broccoli, spinach, and olive oil are best; wheat, corn, and dairy are to be avoided.
2. Those with type A blood should choose fruit, vegetables, tofu, seafood, turkey, and whole grains but avoid meat. For weight loss, seafood, vegetables, pineapple, olive oil, and soy are best; dairy, wheat, corn, and kidney beans should be avoided.
3. Those with type B blood should pick a diverse diet that includes meat, fruit, dairy, seafood, and grains. To lose weight, type B individuals should choose green vegetables, eggs, liver, and licorice tea but avoid chicken, corn, peanuts, and wheat.
4. Those with type AB blood should eat dairy, tofu, lamb, fish, grains, fruit, and vegetables. For weight loss, tofu, seafood, green vegetables, and kelp are best, but chicken, corn, buckwheat, and kidney beans should be avoided.

Keto

Most people nowadays are familiar with the keto diet, which is broken down to keto acidosis and that's a state where the body is out of control; diabetes is out of control, blood glucose goes through the roof, insulin is not able to keep up with his glucose derangement. And so that's a life-threatening state when your type 2 diabetic's body is out of control. Nutritional ketosis is quite different. In Ariel blood sugars and absolutely under control. The patient is healthy in every single way. Electrolytes, insulin, and glucose perfectly controlled. We have now trained the body to switch over from burning carbohydrates as the primary fuel. Now the individual becomes fat adapted, and they use that as the primary source of energy. And that's really the difference between a very unhealthy and a very healthy state.

Here are the most common diets I hear almost everyone tell me they have tried at least once:

1. The Paleo diet. The paleo diet claims that you should eat the same foods that your hunter-gatherer ancestors ate before agriculture developed.
2. The vegan diet. Plant-based only.
3. Low-carb diets. No or less carbs.
4. The Dukan diet. The Dukan diet is a high-protein, low-carbohydrate eating plan designed by Pierre Dukan, a former French physician and self-proclaimed nutritionist. Also called the Dukan method, this diet is based on how hunter-gatherers may have eaten. The diet includes a hundred foods, and all are either proteins or vegetables.
5. The ultra-low-fat diet. An ultra-low-fat (or very low-fat) diet allows for no more than 10 percent of calories from fat. It also tends to be low in protein and very high in carbs with about 10 percent and 80 percent of daily calories, respectively.
6. The Atkins diet. The Atkins diet is a low-carbohydrate fad diet devised by Robert Atkins. The diet is marketed with questionable claims that carbohydrate restriction is crucial to weight loss. There is no good evidence of the diet's effectiveness in achieving durable weight loss, and it may increase the risk of heart disease.
7. The HCG diet. The HCG diet is a weight-loss plan that combines daily injections of human chorionic gonadotropin (HCG) with severe calorie restriction—only five hundred calories per day. HCG is a hormone that's released in large quantities during pregnancy and can be extracted from the urine of pregnant women.

Each of these diets are good in more ways than one. Again, I go back to saying this depends on your body, your age, and your current health state. For instance, I would never give an overweight teenager a vegan diet or a keto diet without knowing their blood type. That being said, I do think it's very possible to practice more than one diet at a time. After all, diet should become a lifestyle. In my house, we never eat out Monday through Friday, and even when we eat out, we are very specific on places we go. We are not vegans; we enjoy plenty of fish in the King household.

Remember, a healthy diet prevents malnutrition and protects from diseases like obesity, heart disease, diabetes, cancer, and stroke. Today many people's diets consist of more saturated fat, trans fats, sugars, and sodium than fruits, vegetables, and dietary fiber. Your body's health reflects what you put into it. I compare food to gasoline in your car. Do you want an 89 or a 91? Always hydrate throughout the day, but never the lowboy the little gray. It can be anything from processed meats to processed snacks, crackers, pretzels, and chips. Those are all in the grocery store in the inside area. Remember, everything at the perimeter of the store that's colorful (vegetables, meats) are all the most important items to a healthy lifestyle.

CHAPTER 6

Pregnant, Nursing, Transitioning

I still recall the very first day I found out I was pregnant and expecting my firstborn son at the age of thirty-one. I thought, *Well, at least I'm out of my twenties.* I know I'm a fit mother. I've been married five years, and I've traveled the world. Now it's time for me to put my focus and attention on being the best mother possible. I began reading every book I could get my hands on to try and prepare. Below are some of the top strategies to help you prepare when expecting; however, you are never prepared. It feels like they throw you in a hot tub of water, and once you get in, it's not so hot but so rewarding. It is actually the most rewarding and best feeling in the world becoming a mom. The four books below were extremely informative:

1. *What to Expect When You're Expecting*
2. Best for first-time moms: *50 Things to Do Before You Deliver*
3. Best for medical information: *Mayo Clinic Guide to a Healthy Pregnancy*
4. Best for rebels: *Expecting Better*

However, it's nothing like somebody handing you a person and saying, "You have to do everything for this person. They're completely depending on you for everything and anything, and you can get no sleep. However, you still have to take care of yourself because to take care of a baby, you actually have to be healthy and strong in order to do it." So it's really tricky. Although I did go into motherhood understanding that I have to continue to take care of my family, cook, clean, feed the baby, and feed myself. All those times I skipped meals, I realized that was the worst thing I could do because I was producing so much milk. Weight was falling off so fast, and I wasn't ever hungry because I was moving so fast and doing so much. You see, we are called woman for a reason. We are born with wings. If we can have babies. We can do anything. Everything we touch is blessed. So if you're pregnant or trying to conceive, remember that patience is a virtue. Remember that God's time is a perfect time because he knows when you are ready for that challenge. Remember, motherhood changes every aspect of your life including one of the most important things: sleep. I remember the time I took the baby to his one-week checkup. I walked in and just started to cry. I totally forgot everything I read, or maybe I didn't forget. Maybe I was just overwhelmed and suffering from a very severe case of sleep deprivation. See, my baby was born at 4:00 a.m., so he would sleep during the day and stay up all night. By the time I learned how to sleep train, it was too late.

I have a very close friend of mine, Britany Bell CEO of (The Mama Gang), who definitely guided me through those first couple of weeks. I don't think I would've been able to make it, so remember that sisterhood is vital when transitioning into motherhood because you need support other than your spouse, your mate, your husband, or your partner, someone else who's already gone through or about to go through what you are going through. Every piece of advice is a gift. Once you get on a schedule, it takes six to eight weeks to really have a routine and start getting to know your body because your body changes so much—your metabolism, your immune system, your energy levels. I found that taking a meal replacement shake or even simply a vegan Muscle Milk or protein shakes allows me to make sure I'm feeding the baby the proper nutrients without becoming gassy, hungry, and depriving myself but also losing weight and making sure I get all the nutrients my body needs. I also did that for six months of pregnancy. At night I couldn't go to sleep without a protein shake. I bought vegan Muscle Milk in chocolate. Is was the only one that I would drink every night before bed, and my baby came out twenty-one and a half inches and weighing 8 pounds and one ounce of muscle. I would strongly advise this for every mom. I was 125 pounds before I got pregnant. By the time I got to the hospital to deliver the baby, I was 168 pounds. I nursed my son for two years, but after four months, I had my six-pack back. I had lost all of the baby weight and more. I was actually skinnier postpartum than I was before I had the baby, the reason being I was so active nursing around the clock. And believe it or not, my favorite dinner was cream of wheat made with almond milk and cinnamon I believe that had a lot to do with it. I don't know why, but nursing was burning so many calories. I would just crave for some warm cream of wheat. I did that for a year, and now I don't like it as much. It's crazy how postpartum your taste buds change. Your body changes, and the baby actually enjoys some of the same foods that you've eaten during pregnancy. One fascinating area of research highlights the way in which infants may be able to detect tastes in human breast milk. In other words, your baby can actually taste what you are eating. Which is not surprising, really, considering they started tasting those flavors while in the amniotic fluid. Not only do your taste buds change, your body changes so much not just by the shape you gain or what weight you lose.

I find it so fascinating that God is so powerful even to the simplest form of the baby knowing the smell of their mother. While you're breastfeeding, it's known that your body will emit a stronger smell than normal through your underarm sweat to help your baby find its source of food. This is your body's response to naturally assist your baby in finding the breast, and it will begin right after giving birth. Now, isn't that just simply powerful? It is also proven in your sense of smell. For many women, sensitivity to strong (and sometimes icky) smells starts to subside fairly quickly and early in pregnancy. If it doesn't, your nose will likely return to normal as pregnancy progresses or soon after delivery. As your hormones begin to settle down in the second trimester, your taste buds should return to normal. However, if you're like me, it will take some time. While I was nursing, I realized I didn't want to eat the foods I ate while I was pregnant. I craved for Thai noodles with my go-to: pickles. I didn't even want to see or smell those things anymore after giving birth to the baby. It's fascinating how different every woman's body is. I love that if we were all the same, life would be so boring.

CHAPTER 7

Comfort Food

When I think of comfort, I think of my bed. My bed is one of the most comfortable places in the world, especially in the arms of my husband. Our bodies are fascinating. What we put in our bodies affects our energy throughout the day, our brain, and the amount of activity are able to endure. I'll give you an example. I usually eat soup and salad. I'm extremely disciplined. Monday through Friday, I cook every day. On Saturdays and Sundays, I sometimes will go out. Usually I'll cook Sunday dinner and meal prep for the week ahead; however, on one Saturday afternoon, we went shopping at the Camarillo Outlet. I worked out earlier that morning with my butt zoology girl group hard. My husband kept saying, "There is nothing else open to eat. We can get a chicken cheesesteak." I said, "Okay, I'll try it." I took a bite of a sandwich and realized I was starving. I went back into the food court and purchased half a sandwich. I ate half a sandwich and passed out within ten minutes. I realized then that comfort food is real. Especially for someone like me who never stepped outside of those boundaries and really eat bread or any type of fast food/processed anything. I was in the backseat of the Escalade, knocked out. My husband was laughing; everyone was cracking up. They had never seen me have the Idis. After that experience, I was a believer. It's proven there are chemicals in fast food that balance out your serotonin levels and can make you tired.

"And when blood volume goes down in the brain, we get woozy and tired." According to Levitsky, eating triggers your parasympathetic nervous system, which conserves energy and slows down your heart rate to absorb nutrients. "It's got to be a large meal with some serous carbohydrates and or oils." Here are some foods that make you tired:

1. Pasta. Yes, the carbs give you a jolt of energy, but "eating refined carbohydrates like pasta can cause a rise in blood sugar, followed by a plunge in insulin levels, which can cause fatigue and weakness.
2. Bananas.
3. Red meat.
4. Cherries.
5. Salmon.
6. Lettuce.

You see, even healthy foods can make you tired.

Eating too much saturated fat in particular increases your blood levels of (LDL) cholesterol and raises your risk for heart disease. Other typical comfort food ingredients are refined carbohydrates (such as those found in white flour, noodles, or white rice) and, of course, sugar.

I never eat after seven o'clock at night. Well, unless I'm pregnant, that is. And even then, I have a protein shake. I remember that Muscle Milk used to help me and the baby sleep. I found that sleeping on empty or full stomach is not good. While it's not recommend to sleep on an empty stomach we also suggest you avoid sleeping on a full stomach. It can have an adverse effect on your insulin levels, which spikes your blood sugar and can lead to weight gain.

Eating comfort foods or junk foods can create a quick spike in your blood sugar. Eating junk foods high in refined carbohydrates and added sugars can cause a surge in insulin, leading to a quick drop in blood sugar. That leaves you feeling tired, cranky, and hungry for more. Just one serving of junk food can increase inflammation throughout your body. These foods can keep you feeling weak, tired, sluggish, and horrible afterward and increase fatigue throughout the day:

1. Sugary foods including syrup and honey
2. White bread
3. Baked goods
4. Highly caffeinated drinks
5. Heavily processed foods such as potato chips

If you're diabetic or if someone with prediabetes, type 1, or type 2 diabetes feels tired after eating, it could be a symptom of hyperglycemia or hypoglycemia. Hyperglycemia (high blood sugar) may occur when too much sugar is consumed.

If you have a hard time going to the bathroom after eating your favorite comfort food, then please drink some warm water with lemon. Hydrate so your body can flush itself out. For most people with digestive complaints such as irritable bowel syndrome (IBS), chronic pancreatitis, or a stomach bug, high levels of fatty foods may trigger stomach pain, cramping, and diarrhea. Greasy meals delay stomach emptying and may cause bloating, nausea, and stomach pain.

Most people don't believe that the stomach can actually explode. Well, truth be told, it can "explode" from eating too much. You probably won't, but the possibility exists. The average human stomach holds about one liter's worth of content. You might have heard that the stomach can shrink or stretch, and to a certain degree, that's true. However, if you eat too much and if you eat too quickly, you'll have overeaten by the time your body gets the fullness signal. Also, try to listen to your body when you get that full feeling. Get moving. If you've overeaten, take a gentle walk to help stimulate the process in your body that pushes the food down your gastrointestinal track. If you have a stomach ache, you can apply a heating pad, hot water bottle, hot towel, or heat wrap over the abdomen and back. This helps relax the muscles in the abdomen and relieve abdominal cramps and pain. The temperature should ideally be 104 degrees Fahrenheit.

Taking a hot bath with bubbles and essential oils or hot showers can also help. I remember when I would not eat very much, I would be moody and sleepy, and I thought I was doing the right thing to lose weight. See, we must be careful with training our stomach. It can shrink and expand, but listen to your body. If you're hungry, eat. Something clean, of course, but do eat. Here are some ways you still can enjoy comfort food. Try these healthy alternatives to traditional comfort foods:

1. Get creative with pizza crusts and toppings.
2. Use alternative pasta and sneak in extra veggies for a healthier macaroni and cheese.
3. Enjoy a fully loaded baked sweet potato.
4. Try a new take on tacos. Which is my favorite. I'm in love with Mexican food; I love *pico de gallo*, and I love sour cream. So usually on my cheat day, I'm craving fajitas or nachos with shrimp.

In terms of grading the food that we eat, fried animal products (that would be stuff like fast food, you know, like burgers, french fries, hotdogs, etc.) get in a grade of F. The next is animal products, and these would be chicken, beef, pork, turkey, lamb, eggs, and all of the dairy. We would still have to give these an F. And then there's processed junk; that would be chips, cookies, cakes, ice cream, candy, and chocolates. We will give them a D. The next would be sodas, coffee, and oils (olive, canola, palm, peanut, flax, vegetable, coconut) and all your Sotos that are sweetened. We would also give this a D. And then there is plant-based junk: soy dog, soy trail bars, veggie burgers, soy rice. I would give this a C-minus. And then there are plant-based processed foods. What are they? By processed I mean refined grains like bread, oat milk, soy milk, rice milk, sorbet, and no-oil sauces and dressings. And we would give this a B. And then last but not least, whole plant foods. Those are rice, quinoa, oats, sweet berries, barley, root vegetables, all your greens (kale, collards, chard), legumes, and all your beans. We would give this an A-plus.

So what do they mean by whole plant-based food? In front of me I have apple juice, applesauce, and an apple. Juice is mostly sugar and is very processed. When consumed, our bodies are forced to deal with this surge of sugar in a normal state of shock. To put it simply, it's hard on our system. Into our body goes some fiber. Almost all the fiber has already been processed, so it has very little benefit. Then there is the apple in its whole form. When consumed, our teeth benefit from the skin in terms of cleaning. The time it takes for us to chew and swallow the apple gives ample time for our bodies to prepare and break it down over a longer period. The sugar is released slowly as well, and our bodies have time to absorb all the nutrients much more efficiently. This is also a great example of what they mean by processing foods. Many fruits are low in calories yet rich in fiber, which may benefit weight loss. Some fruits, including apples, berries, and melons, may also increase feelings of fullness.

Fruit is nature's ready-made snack, packed with vitamins, fiber, and other nutrients that support a healthy diet.

Fruit is also generally low in calories and high in fiber, which may help you lose weight.

In fact, eating fruit is linked to a lower body weight and a lower risk of diabetes, high blood pressure, cancer, and heart disease. My favorite fruits for weight loss are grapefruit, Pomelo oranges, apples, berries, and cherries.

There was a time when protein shakes would have fifty to a hundred grams of protein per shake. It wasn't until this study came out that it was determined that per meal, we can only ingest twenty to thirty grams of protein every three to four hours. Every person varies on timing and needs. Instead of having two chicken breasts per meal (which has approximately sixty-two grams of protein), have one chicken breast per meal (thirty-one grams). Eating a slice of bread is not the same as eating four cups of sweet potatoes. Simple carbs are digested quicker by the body, leaving you hungry. However, complex carbs take time for the body to digest.

Simples carbs are found in food such as fruits, milk, soft drinks and more. Complex carbs are found in foods such as whole grains, beans, vegetables, and more.

Simple and complex carbs serve different purposes.

Eating simple carbs is recommended before starting a workout if you have not eaten anything for the past two to four hours. This way you have a boost of energy.

Eating complex carbs is recommended at least thirty to forty-five minutes after a workout so you can replenish your glycogen levels. Eating this way, you will feel satisfied after workouts, so there is no craving.

It's not only about doing abdominal workouts and cardio. It's about hitting all muscle groups two to five times a week for significant impact in the body. Beginners should start with compound movements (which target more than one muscle group).

A simple guideline would be one to three sets of eight to twelve repetitions with a thirty-second to a one-minute-and-a-half break in between sets.

Squats target the lower body while the glute bridges primarily target the glutes and hamstrings. Dead-stop pushups target the upper body (front), and downward dog targets the upper back.

All exercises below target the core muscle, which is why I love to leave the plank for last. The plank targets all muscle groups if done correctly.

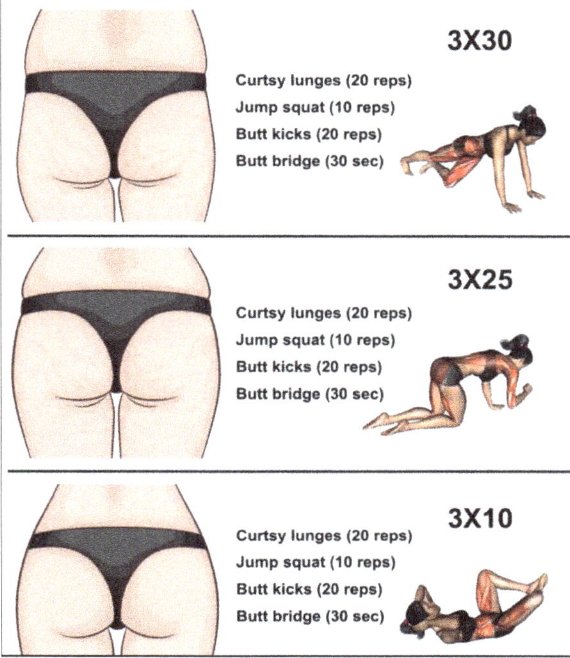

It's not bad to break your diet from time to time. After all, we're humans! The problem is when we overindulge ourselves.

Everything in proportion.

Planning for one cheat meal a week will not cause major impacts to the body with regard to gaining weight. However, a cheat day will have an impact on the body to gaining weight and feeling bloated.

If your body is accustomed to eating at certain times during the day but you skip a meal, the body identifies this as something in the body is changing; therefore, the next meal you decide to have will be stored in our bodies as fat as a means to survive.

Unless you're doing intermittent fasting, you shouldn't skip meals. Even then, you have to know what foods to eat so the body does not store it as fat.

What you shouldn't do is skip a meal for weight loss purposes. What you should do is plan out the meals and snacks you're going to eat for the day or week and focus on portion control, balancing your proteins, carbs and fats, and drinking lots of water. I talked about hydration in the previous chapter, but I can't stress this to you enough. Hydration is far more important than anything we can think of. Water, rest, veggies, fruits, protein, grains, and seeds are what you can live on. Without all of these, your body is lacking something and chemically imbalanced.

We need to be aware of the amount of food we put on our plate. There needs to be a healthy portion of carbs, fats, and protein on our plates.

Instead of having 85 percent of your plate full of pasta (carbs), only put in 35 percent. Fill the rest up with as much green vegetables as you desire then have 40 percent of protein (chicken breast) and 25 percent of fat (avocado).

Below you will find an example of a portioned meal:

It is vital that we get enough rest. My husband always tells me I need my beauty sleep, and the older I get the more I listen to my body. I never realized that for your body to heal and remain healthy, you need adequate sleep. I can't believe that I used to sleep four hours, run around all day and night, party, wake up, work out, help my grandfather, eat crackers or cereal, and repeat. The body is a living organism and needs to remain healthy and get its much-needed rest.

The body needs to recover and process everything that it has gone through throughout the day. Not only does sleeping help you fight night cravings, but it also helps to increase physical activity output because you're well rested.

Can't sleep at night? Here are a few solutions:

1. Don't bring your phone to the bedroom.
2. Put a timer so you can remind yourself to go to bed early.
3. Don't eat anything heavy before going to bed.

Sleep is one of the most important parts of having great health in life. I remember when the pandemic first started, I thought I would get loads of sleep. But being a mother, a wife, and a business owner having to work from home, I found it was even more complex. I wasn't able to sleep. Never allow worry to make you lose your sleep. Never allow any distractions around to stop you from getting your rest. After all, you know we ladies we need our beauty rest. I still need to work on this area because I'm always busy helping family-run businesses or cooking and cleaning. The older I get, the more I realize rest is medicine just as food is.

We have the ability to change our lives by putting our health first because health is wealth.

CHAPTER 8

Hydration: Water Is Life

What or when or where can I start? I feel like God created water because water was healing. What is the only thing that can really put out fire? Water is the most powerful component that God created. In the beginning of the book, I explained the time when I was hospitalized for dehydration and exhaustion. When my face swole up, that would've never happened had I been hydrated. All seven trillion cells in your body form healthy or unhealthy, and water is the cause of it either way. If your body is having trouble maintaining blood pressure, it slows blood flow to nonvital organs such as your kidneys and gut to survive, causing damage. Without your kidneys filtering your blood, cellular waste quickly builds up. You're literally dying for a glass of water.

Meanwhile, many people have passed away from dehydration. The easiest way to make yourself accountable is to take a gallon of water with you everywhere you go. I never leave my house without my gallon of water even if I'm just going to the grocery store. Once got held me from exhaustion, and my face swelled up. My body was never the same. Whenever my mouth feels dry, I rinse it out with freshly squeezed lemon and just drink lots of water. Remember, we can live without food for weeks but we can't live more than a few days without water.

As a general rule of thumb, a person can survive without water for about three days. However, some factors such as how much water an individual body needs and how it uses water can affect this. Factors that may change how much water a person needs include age and weight. Water also helps suppress appetite. If you're hydrated, you will not pray for those processed snacks like crackers and chips and pretzels. Water tricks your brain and makes you think that you're full so you don't eat as much. Every morning when I wake up, I take a cup of warm lemon water just to flush out my kidneys from the day before. People always ask me why I drink room-temperature water. It is because I'm a singer, and I don't like anything too cold or too hot. However, I prefer warm, really warm. I can drink hot tea in 100° weather.

Dehydration is the worst feeling ever. Here are some ways to check if you're hydrated or not:

1. Coolness. Hands, arms, feet, and legs may be increasingly cool to the touch.
2. Confusion. The patient may not know the time or place and may not be able to identify people around them.
3. Incontinence.
4. Restlessness.
5. Congestion.
6. Urine decrease.
7. Fluid and food decrease.

If you ever have any of these symptoms, hydrate. I say hydrate anyways. I'll be honest. All I drink is hot tea or water. I've trained myself over the years. Juice is high in sugar, and soda is just a no-no. Unless I'm sick with an upset, stomach or pregnant. I will drink ginger beer or ginger ale until about five months of pregnancy. I wanted my baby to have a lot of hair, so I stayed with the heartburn. I have to drink ginger ale to release the gas in my belly, but other than that, water is my go-to.

CHAPTER 9

Bunsology Body Workout: Lifestyle

What burns the most calories in thirty minutes?

Ideally on this situation, we would be able to get you doing a movement that engages your full body. When you are able to run with efficiency and intensity, this would be our best fat burner. The moment I was given the okay from my doctor postpartum, I was ready to get back to full-body exercise and cardio. I just felt so lazy and heavy and even more tired without working out. Getting those sprints on the tracks (or treadmill, alternatively) in the sun and really getting that heart rate up there would be ideal.

If you're just starting, we are going to get you onto those mats and firing up those knees, getting those mountain climbers on. Same thing, same concept: really getting that heart rate up and making sure you're sweating. Either or will be equally as effective, especially when starting to work your way into it and melting that fat off!

Ten Best HIIT Workout Combinations to Burn Calories Fast

Combo 1.

1.   High knees (20 seconds work, 40 seconds rest, 5 sets)
2.   Plank jacks (20 seconds work, 40 seconds rest, 5 sets)
3.   Burpees (30 seconds work, 60 seconds rest, 4 sets)

Combo 2.

1.   Side plank walks (30 seconds work, 60 seconds rest, 5 sets)
2.   Jumping lunges (20 seconds work, 40 seconds rest, 5 sets)
3.   Mountain climbers (20 seconds work, 40 seconds rest, 5 sets)

Combo 3.

1.   Jump squats (20 seconds work, 40 seconds rest, 5 sets)
2.   Plank jacks (20 seconds work, 40 seconds rest, 5 sets)
3.   High knees (30 seconds work, 60 seconds rest, 5 sets)

Combo 4.

1.   Side lunges (30 seconds work, 60 seconds rest, 5 sets)
2.   Saw plank (30 seconds work, 60 seconds rest, 5 sets)
3.   Butt kick (30 seconds work, 60 seconds rest, 5 sets)

Combo 5.

1.   Side plank walks (30 seconds work, 60 seconds rest, 5 sets)
2.   Burpees (30 seconds work, 60 seconds rest, 5 sets)
3.   High knees (30 seconds work, 60 seconds rest, 5 sets)

Combo 6.

1. Set A
   a. 4 sets of 100 jumping jacks/jump rope/high knees
   b. 4 sets of 25 pushups to burpees
   c. 4 sets of 50 squat jumps
   d. 4 sets of 1-minute plank twist or hold sit-ups
2. Set B
   a. Jumping jacks (20 seconds work)
   b. Mountain climbers (20 seconds work)
   c. 60-seconds rest
3. Set C (4 sets)
   a. Side plank walks (20 seconds work)
   b. Saw plank (20 seconds work)
   c. Burpees (20 seconds work)
   d. 90-second rest

Combo 7.

1. Set A (4 sets)
   a. Dumbbell Squats (30 seconds work)
   b. Side Squats (30 seconds work)
   c. 60-second rest
2. Set B (4 sets)
   a. High knees (30 seconds work)
   b. Butt kick (30 seconds work)
   c. Burpees (20 seconds work)
   d. 90-second rest

Combo 8.

1. Set A (4 sets)
   a. Jumping lunges (20 seconds work)
   b. Mountain climbers (20 seconds work)
   c. 60-second rest

2. Set B (4 sets)
    a. Jumping jacks (30 seconds work)
    b. Side squats (30 seconds work)
    c. High knees (20 seconds work)
    d. 90-second rest

Combo 9.

Set A (4 sets)
    a. Squat jumps (20 seconds work)
    b. Jumping jacks (20 seconds work)
    c. 60-seconds rest

Set B (4 sets)
    a. Mountain climbers (20 seconds work)
    b. Side plank Walks (20 seconds work)
    c. Saw plank (20 seconds work)
    d. 90-second rest

Combo 10.

Set A (4 sets)
    a. Jumping jacks (30 seconds work)
    b. High knees (20 seconds work)
    c. Butt kick (20 seconds work)
    d. 60-second rest

Set B (4 sets)
    a. Burpees (30 seconds work)
    b. Mountain climbers (30 seconds work)
    c. 90-second rest

CHAPTER 10

Detox Mind, Body, and Soul

Detoxes are usually best when you have to shock your body. By doing a detox or minimizing the toxins your body has to process, you give your liver the space it needs to start processing these toxins again. Once processed, they are released into the lymphatic system, kidneys, and blood to be eliminated. Most people detox or cleanse for quick weight loss. I usually detox every quarter (every three months) because I noticed that my skin tends to break out when the seasons change or I'm dehydrated. Most detox diets are generally short-term dietary interventions designed to eliminate toxins from your body. A typical detox diet involves a period of fasting followed by a strict diet of fruit, vegetables, fruit juices, and water. Sometimes a detox also includes herbs, teas, supplements, and colon cleanses or enemas.

I have never used the enema, but I do get a colonics twice a year. Remember, when you're eating clean, it becomes a lifestyle, and you no longer want to eat the fast foods that weigh you down, pile on pounds, and make you gain weight and feel tired. I learned that before you detox, it's best to do it when you're close to your bathroom and bed. You may have to do a number two and urinate much more than usual. If your goal is weight loss, a detox diet might help you drop a few pounds, but you'll likely just gain it back. In the end, you wouldn't have accomplished anything, and it's certainly not a healthy approach. If your goal is to detox your system, don't waste your time or money. Actually, complete your detox and then make lifestyle changes so that you don't gain the weight back. The top weight loss detox recipes are

1. lemon and mint detox water (Lemon is the most used fruit during summers.);
2. cucumber detox water;
3. apple and cinnamon detox water;
4. grapefruit detox water;
5. orange detox water.

They all work, but if you're not careful, you will definitely gain back more weight later. After a full-body detox, here are a few ways to rejuvenate your body:

1. Common misconceptions about detoxing. Detox diets are said to eliminate toxins from your body, improve health, and promote weight loss.
2. Limit alcohol.
3. Focus on sleep.
4. Drink more water.
5. Reduce your intake of sugar and processed foods.
6. Eat antioxidant-rich foods.
7. Eat foods high in probiotics.
8. Decrease your salt intake.

All of the following will help you get back on track and allow your body to process its healthy red and white blood cells quicker. You will poop more than normal. This is why I say detox when you can be home near your bathroom. If you experience green stools during a colon cleanse, it may be due to food rushing through your intestines too quickly to allow bacteria to give your stool its characteristic brown color. A high-fat diet like the keto diet may give your poop a bright green color. When detoxing, it will seem like you urinate every hour. Your urine will be darkest when your issue is water retention. Dark-colored, cloudy, strong-smelling urine is normal in the first few days of your detox. As you get toward the last few days, it will clear up and look more like water. If you follow your detox perfectly, the diet, aimed at people wanting to lose a lot of weight, claims you'll drop up to ten pounds if you follow it for three days. Every morning whether you're detoxing or not, you should consume one of these five simple morning drinks to melt belly fat:

1. Jeera water. Jeera is a must-use spice in all Indian curries.
2. Saunf water.
3. Ajwain water.
4. Lemon water.
5. Green tea.

CHAPTER 11

Healthy Body, Healthy Relationships
God's Heart, God's Grace

I start out each and every day in prayer. I'm not going to lie. I need to work on meditation. Being able to block out everything that is going on around you, all the noise all the distractions, and simply focusing on that moment in time has such power in it. I remember the first time I went to a professional meditation session that I loved, and I felt so rejuvenated. As if I just did a complete physical workout, my body was drained and my brain felt like it had worked overtime. However, this feeling is what's priceless; it's a feeling that I really can't describe in words.

Lord, thank you for giving me an example
of a virtuous woman through your Word. In your
wisdom, you've already laid out what she looks
like and who she is. Mostly, though, thank you
for allowing me to see that being a Proverbs 31
woman isn't about my deeds but my character.

I'll admit that prior to now, I was overwhelmed and felt daunted by all the things the Proverbs 31 woman did. It's comforting to know my focus should be on developing godly character instead.

Also, help me to teach my children the godly attributes they should look for in a spouse. I want them to marry a godly spouse and not be unequally yoked with an unbeliever.

Groom my heart to desire godly character over good deeds because I know godly character will eventually produce good, godly deeds.

Bring other women into my life who will disciple me as Proverbs 31 woman. And bring women into my life who I can link arms with and with whom we can hold each accountable. Amen.

Affirmation and Confession. This is vital and, I believe, the most important part of life: continuing to encourage yourself in the Lord. I feel like that great health as a woman and as a wife as well. As a Proverbs 31 woman, we must all remember to encourage ourselves. I've learned over the years that nobody will love you like God and nobody on earth can love you unless you love yourself first. Before I was married, I only had two really serious relationships. I found that my inner health, which was my diet and nutrition, was just as important as my outer appearance because beauty is deceitful and temporary, but your heart being pure and true is eternal. A wonderful way to start your new year is to complete twenty-one days of fasting and praying. I know this may seem hard or complex if you've never heard of what proper fasting means. There are different forms of fasting: the Daniel fast, liquid/water fasting, intermittent fasting, and the list goes on. Most importantly, remember that fasting is the sacrifice part; whenever you feel hungry, just continue to manifest scripture and positive things over your life and yourself. Manifest the things you wish to obtain or wish to accomplish as if they were already in your world. While you're fasting, remember to continue to pray and hydrate. You can completely surrender to God in all you are and all you do. Remember, overall health is internal first.

> She opens her mouth with wisdom, And on her tongue is the law of kindness. She watches over the ways of her household, And does not eat the bread of idleness. (Proverbs 31:26–27)

Remember to use your mouths to speak wisdom, life, and kindness. The words we speak are *powerful!* And we should use them to glorify God by encouraging, inspiring, and edifying others.

> Lord, help me be well organized so my household can be well prepared for their tasks and our home can be efficient and well-run. I understand that this is not only a blessing to my family but to those who may come alongside to help me in different areas or seasons of my life.
>
> Also, help me to recognize when I need help, to be a humble enough to ask for help. This will also lessen my load and give me greater freedom to flow in other areas of my life and home. Sometimes I struggle to ask for help. So help me see that asking for help isn't a sign of weakness, that it's a sign of strength and humility. I have no need to feel shame or embarrassment. Please bring people into my life who I can trust and who will be loyal to me during those times of help. Not people who will expose or mock me.
>
> Lord, I need the wisdom to know who I should ask for help. At the same time, I want to be open to the help I receive. Amen.

I am well organized.
I am productive.

I run an efficient home.

I know how to delegate tasks to the best person who can get the job done.

I am not ashamed to ask for help because help is a gift to me. It frees me up to be productive in other areas of my life.

I have wisdom and a keen eye to know who is trustworthy and loyal to ask for help. I decree and declare this over my life as according to Proverbs 31:15.

> Lord, help me use my mouth to speak wisdom, life, and kindness. I desire for my words to be purposeful and to tell of my character and godliness.
>
> I refuse to gossip, backbite, slander, or compare myself to others. I want to change the narrative that women are catty, "nice-nasty" toward one another, and can't get along. That's simply not true.
>
> Please surround with me godly women who choose to operate in the Proverbs 31 woman way. If nothing else, please use me to bless other women with my words.
>
> Also, I don't want to eat the bread of idleness. I want to be so caught up in Jesus and God's plans for my life that being idle or a busybody is a not a factor. That's a distraction to my calling and purpose. It's an injustice to my family, the body of Christ, and the kingdom of God.
>
> I want to walk as the godly, virtuous Proverbs 31 woman you've called me to be! In Jesus's name I pray. Amen.

My mouth speaks wisdom, life, and kindness.

My words are purposeful and tell of my character and godliness. I do not gossip, backbite, slander, or compare myself to others.

I am changing the negative narrative of women into the godly, holy, and righteous purpose of women.

I am not idle; I am a busybody. I am so caught up in Jesus and God's plans for my life that there is no time to waste on nonessential activities or conversations.

I am a purposeful and intentional encourager of women.

My words give life and speak to the virtue of every woman I encounter. I decree and declare this over my life as according to Proverbs 31:26–27.

I am a Proverbs 31 woman.

My character is being fully groomed and developed as a good, godly character.

I walk virtuously in all I do as a woman, wife, mother, friend, sister, daughter, homemaker, employee, and business owner.

I am keen on teaching my sons and daughters about the kind of spouse they should marry. They will marry good, godly spouses who have the heart of Jesus.

Godly women are in my life to mentor, discipline, and hold me accountable. I do the same for them.

I decree and declare this over my life as according to Proverbs 31:10–31. And it is so. Amen.

I have attached all these prayers in a book for nutrition because great health involves the mind, body, and soul. Remember, self-care is not selfish. You must remember to take out time for yourself. It is very easy to get caught up in being a girlfriend, a mother, a wife, and working that you forget about yourself. You are the center of it all and the gas in the tank to keep everything moving, so remember to take out time for yourself.

> Lord, help me to go to great lengths to nourish, nurture, and tend to the needs of my family. Help me take care of the precious hearts and souls you've entrusted to me. I desire to be a woman who always has the best interests of my family in mind.

I desire to be like the merchant ships—that I will go to great lengths finding opportunities to access and learn from people not like me and my cultural background. And from there, I will share my culture with them and their culture with my family. Help me develop the character traits of commitment and dedication as the heartbeat of tending to my family. I know this is not based upon my feelings at that particular moment but on love and the desire to meet my family's needs no matter what. Help me keep this holy and righteous perspective. Amen.

ABOUT THE AUTHOR

SouLfia created Bunsology following the passing of her infamous grandfather King Solomon Burke. Not only was he an icon in the music industry; he was the driving force of her purpose and passion in helping others retain everlasting health. She has always been passionate about health and nutrition. Since competing in state pageants at the age of fifteen, marrying NFL cornerback Eric King, and becoming an NASM-certified nutritionist and celebrity personal trainer, SouLfia has proven her skills in healthy weight loss, weight gain, and overall health, including her skills in natural postpartum weight loss.